FIREFIGHTERS
A to Z

CHRIS L. DEMAREST

SCHOLASTIC INC.

New York Toronto London Auckland Sydney
Mexico City New Delhi Hong Kong

To Ethan,
the best little "fighter-fighter" I know

For their passion and enthusiasm and never-ending faith in this project,
I would like to thank Charles Brush, Deputy Chief, Lebanon,
N.H. Fire Department, Trina Schart Hyman, Steve Malk,
and the Meriden Fire Department.

ISBN 0-439-28716-2

12 11 10 9 8 7 6 5 4 3 2 1   1 2 3 4 5 6/0

Printed in the U.S.A.   08

First Scholastic printing, September 2001

Book design by David Caplan
The text of this book is set in HTF Champion.
The illustrations are rendered in pastels.

AUTHOR'S NOTE

Fire is a topic of fascination for most people. The sight of towering flames and the sound of fire engine sirens can be awesome and exciting to those watching from a safe distance. But people underestimate the power of fire. For the people whose job it is to fight fires, fires are dangerous and destructive enemies.

I am an active member of the Meriden, New Hampshire, volunteer fire department. I'm certain that inside every firefighter there is a little bit of the excited boy or girl who loves the shiny trucks, playing with water, and racing to the scene—but when the call is sounded to fight a fire, a firefighter's job is completely serious and focused.

Firefighters A to Z presents a day in the life of a call, or professional, fire department. The strategies and sequence of events in this book would be followed by a volunteer fire department as well. Some major city fire departments can experience thirty calls in one day, but every call is the same: The alarm sounds to call firefighters to action, and at the end of fighting a fire, firefighters rest or sleep in order to be fresh for the next call.

Some of the terms in this book may be unfamiliar. On the *I* page, the *primary search* refers to a firefighting team entering a building to do a quick search to locate and remove any people or animals from the premises. The tank of oxygen on a firefighter's back holds enough air to

Z is for Zip into bed for a rest.

Y is for Yawning. We all did our best.

X is for eXtinguished. We put out the fire.

W is for Water flowing higher and higher.

V is for Ventilate; let gases out.

U is for Up. Black smoke swirls all about.

T is for Teamwork. No one works alone.

S is for Sounding. We test for weak zones.

R is for Rope, hauling tools overhead.

Q is for Quickly, which is how fires spread.

P is for Pickax to make the holes wide.

O is for Opening places fires hide.

N is for Nozzle attached to the hose.

M is for Mask into which clean air flows.

L is for Ladders that rise several floors.

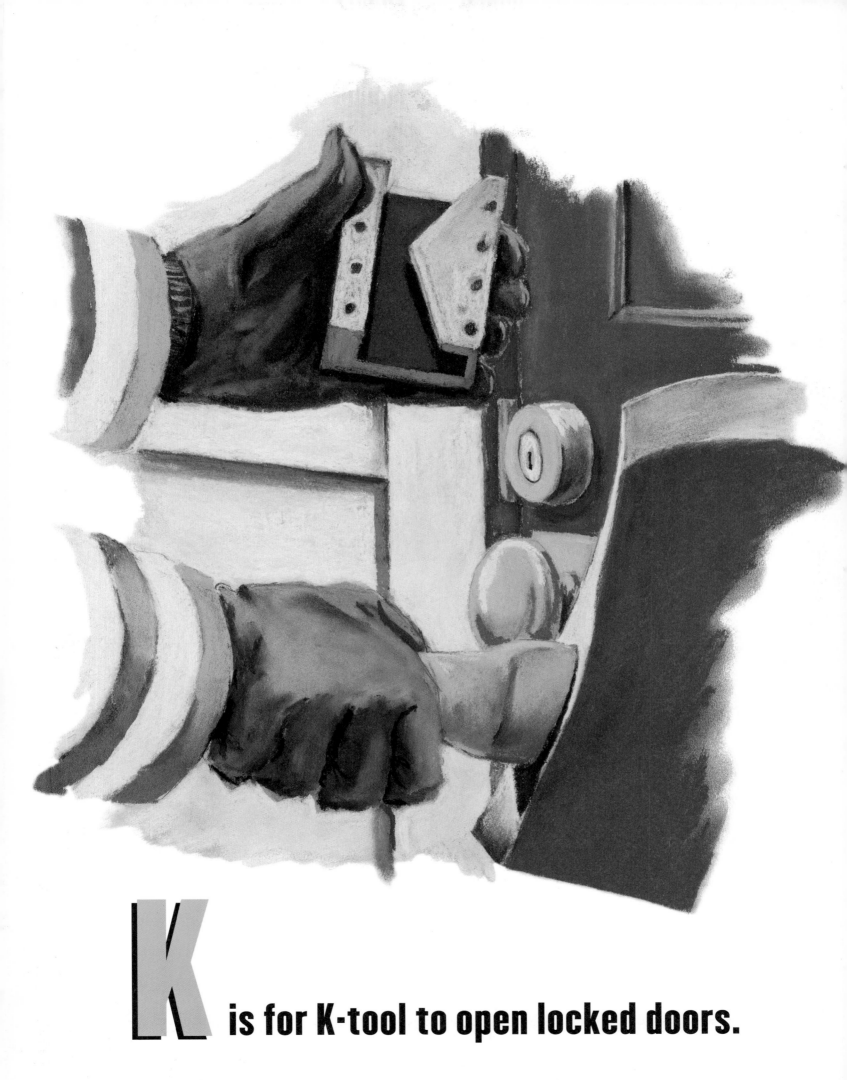

K is for K-tool to open locked doors.

J is for Jump if you feel the floor lurch.

I is for Inside. Start the primary search.

H is for Hoses and Hydrants we need.

G is for Go as we race at full speed.

F is for Fire we see far away.

E is for Engine exiting the bay.

**is for Dalmatian, a firehouse must.**

C is for Chief, whose experience we trust.

B is for Boots stowed in our bunker gear.

A is for Alarm that rings loud and clear.

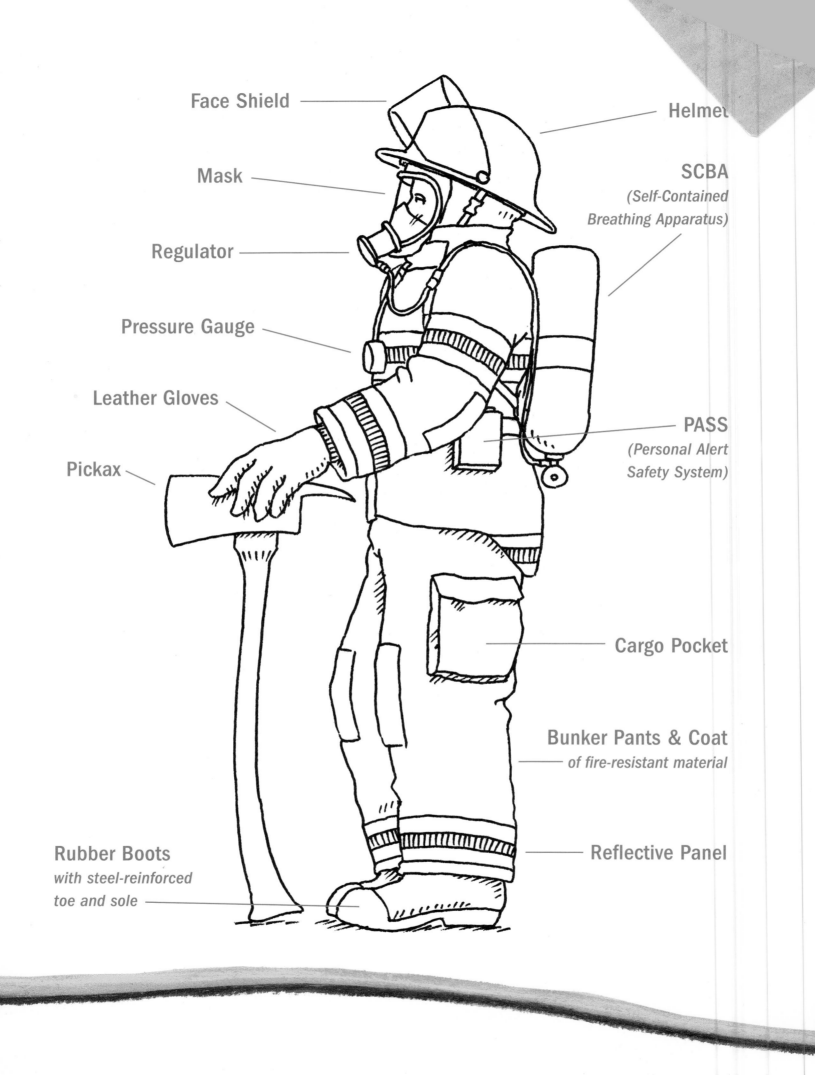

Face Shield

Helmet

Mask

SCBA
*(Self-Contained
Breathing Apparatus)*

Regulator

Pressure Gauge

Leather Gloves

PASS
*(Personal Alert
Safety System)*

Pickax

Cargo Pocket

Bunker Pants & Coat
of fire-resistant material

Rubber Boots
*with steel-reinforced
toe and sole*

Reflective Panel

breathe for thirty minutes, unless the firefighter is working extremely hard in very smoky conditions. Then the oxygen may last for only fifteen minutes. Firefighters don't have much time during a primary search, particularly in a large house or building.

A *K-tool* is a special tool used for removing deadbolt locks from doors. When combined with a hammering tool, the K-tool will pop off a lock, thereby minimizing damage to the door.

Many firefighters have been injured or killed during a fire by falling through floors and roofs that have become weak due to fire or water damage. For safety reasons, firefighters *sound*—or look for weak spots—by bouncing an ax head on a floor or wall. A weakened area will cause the ax to bounce, thereby alerting the firefighter to avoid that spot.

Fire spreads quickly. In less than thirty seconds a small flame can get completely out of control and turn into a major fire. Fire uses up oxygen and produces smoke and poisonous gases that can cause fires to literally explode. To reduce the risk of these fire explosions, it is essential to *ventilate* the fire, to release the explosive gases out into the air.

A firefighter in full gear can take on an almost alien look. Room temperatures in a fire can be 100 degrees at floor level and rise to 600 degrees at eye level. Firefighters wear a helmet, mask, boots, and clothes coated with a material that keeps heat and steam from penetrating and burning the skin. They may look strange, but they will be safe.

Everyone fears fire—even firefighters. According to the United States Fire Administration, each year more than 5,000 Americans die in fires and more than 25,000 are injured. Fire deaths and damage can be reduced by teaching people the basic facts about fire and fire prevention. I hope this book will introduce readers to the serious side of fires and firefighting.

And don't forget—October is National Fire Prevention Month in the United States.

C. L. D.

Meriden, New Hampshire